How not to have
The Life of a Step-Wife

Written by:
Windy Samaria

© Copyright 2023, Windy Samaria
All rights reserved
First Edition

First originally published by Windy Samaria 2023

ISBN 979-8-9885553-0-8 (Paperback)
ISBN 979-8-9885553-1-5 (Digital)

Printed in the United States of America

PREFACE:

First, I do not identify as a relationship expert or a licensed therapist; I am married with children and have experienced my own triumphs and tribulations. I have listened to friends and acquaintances about relationships and some of the struggles associated with some relationships. I wrote this book to help someone in their relationship that can benefit from guidance or encouragement if you are seeking or currently in a relationship. We could use a variety of perspectives of what others have overcome, to get a sense of the path we can take as individuals or as a union. I hope this book will help both women and men have another perspective or understanding of the person in their life, understand how to be a better you, or how you can select someone that compliments you.

This book is dedicated to my parents. My late mother Sarah Davis Jackson, who spent much of her life trying to help others and to my father Carl Jackson Jr. He is the best example of a father that I could have ever hoped for. It has taken me over a decade to gather my thoughts to write this book because I have been following my own journey of life's lessons and learning from others. My parents helped mold me into the woman I am today. Some strengths I have adopted and some shortcomings I have observed and turned them into strengths that works best for me. I do not have all the answers to life or relationships, but I have learned and continue to learn from an innate ability to observe other's successes or areas for growth. One thing that is certain; life and death happens, and it is what we do in between that matters here. We are who we are, and life and its' experiences have a way of shaping the rest of who we become.

This book is also dedicated to everyone in a relationship, seeking a relationship or in between. Some of you may have met your spouse in high school or college where you had time to mature and grow with each other and others either have met or will meet at a bar, gas station, online, blind date, introduced by a friend, friend's wedding, a birthday party, church, or literally anywhere. However, or wherever you meet or going to meet your spouse this self-help book is for you.

Windy Samaria

Table of Contents

Preface

Table of Contents

Definitions of Step-Wife

Thought One – Selfish Behavior

Thought Two – Conditional Love

Thought Three – Immaturity

Thought Four – Single and Married, not Much in Common

Thought Five – Read the Signs

Thought Six – Relationship Interview Questions

Thought Seven – Do not Waste your Life

Thought Eight – Boundaries Anyone?

Thought Nine – Be Alone or Be Lonely

Thought Ten – Being Unequally Yoked

Thought Eleven – No Tricks or Treats

Thought Twelve – Is Sex Overrated?

Thought Thirteen – My Parents Said

Thought Fourteen – You are not Going to Change Him or Her

Thought Fifteen – Secrets or Not

Thought Sixteen – Watch and Listen to Body Language

Thought Seventeen – Eyes Wide Open

Thought Eighteen – Listen to the Silence, you may Hear the Clues

Thought Nineteen – What to Do?

Thought Twenty – Public Service Messages

Thought Twenty-One – Ladies and Gentlemen

Thought Twenty-Two – Say What You Mean and Mean What You Say!

Thought Twenty-Three – Meet in the Middle

Thought Twenty-Four – The Value of your Time

My Closing Thoughts

Special Thanks

My definitions of a Step-wife are:

(a) a woman who is living with a man, acting as a wife and the man will not commit to marriage;
(b) a legal wife who is being treated poorly by her husband. Poorly treated meaning a cheater, or mentally, physically, or emotionally abusive;
(c) the other woman, (aka) "side-chick." Sneaking around to have fun with someone who is not your husband, fiancé, or boyfriend; without the duties that comes with the person with whom you are cheating such as cooking, cleaning, laundry, impromptu back rubs, going to kid's sports practices, him satisfied only sex, or night trips to the store for milk or cold medicine;
(d) a woman who limits her self-worth to accept a man with no job, no goals, no ambitions, not motivated to achieve any goals, drives her car, drops her off at work, at her home playing video games, cheating, hanging out with the guys, will not babysit her kids, or take care their children together, will not clean, will not have dinner ready since he is unemployed, or openly share a man or fight with another woman over a no-good man, just to say that she has a man.

Thought

1

Selfish Behavior

Selfish people seem to be more prevalent these days. Not to say that people have not been selfish all through the years, however, it seems to have increased in professionalism, general humanity, and certainly in relationships. People seem to require that their immediate needs are met without compromising or making any or limited sacrifices. In relationships one should wonder how someone you are committed to can say that they love you and still have selfish behavior, chances are the person that you are committed to does not even know they are acting selfishly and it could be what we have often heard that women and men do not think alike and it is as if we come from different planets. We should show and communicate to our mate what we want from a relationship as an individual rather than a mass of ideas that may or may not have worked for another relationship, because just as sure as we each have different finger prints, we also have different personalities and views. Often, our child rearing evolves into how your child rearing affects you as an adult and consequently as a parent. I have often said and heard others say, "when I have a family, I'm going to do this differently than how my mother or father raised me." and we live on and our children will have different views on how we raised them and will say that they will raise their children differently than how they were raised. It does not necessarily mean the way you were raised was wrong or right way to be raised, some of how we were brought up is our perception to how we were raised which can shape us into who we are, multiply that with someone you are committed too and that is a piece of work with an equally interesting or just plain different upbringing. It is complex when you think about it. I will use my life as an example. I was raised in what I would consider lower middle class. My dad was the main breadwinner or support for my mother, brother, and me. Because we were what I deem a small family with mom, dad and two children we had just about all that we needed and some of the things that we wanted. The values that I learned growing up was radically Biblical based from the spiritual aspect and from a practical aspect the values I learned were to treat others as I wish to be treated, follow the ten commandments, get an education, work, and get married and then have a family. Having that kind of childhood which I would say was extremely structured, made me become structured in some areas and laxer in others, especially with how I view raising my children. Having that type of childhood also made me intrigued with my husband because how he was raised seemed foreign and a world I had only read about. My husband's childhood were many siblings, they did not have all that they needed and rarely what they wanted. They had a rough type of lifestyle. He was equally curious about my life. He once told me that I came from a "Leave it to Beaver" family. We had to overcome our learning curve for one another and try to build our own standards of life for our family, based on what works better or sometimes just shoot for the less confrontational outcome for us, and that is a life-long journey. Add children with their own unique personalities to the mix and the routine repeats generation after generation. The main thing that is constant, is the ability to put oneself last and think of the other person and how they may feel before I say or do anything. That has been quality in people seems to be fading away.

Thought

2

Conditional Love

It seems today, that love is a term most use very loosely, which I find usually mean that it is conditional, and it seems that conditional is the best that many can do these days. They use to say that the men and women of "yesterday" or years ago shared real love, I think it is true to a degree, however, I feel from the conversations that I have had with people of different ages, that conditional love has been around longer than we recognize. Just because we have gone through a thing or two make us as a human race and some feel as though we are the only person who have felt this way or been through any trials or hardships, not true. I heard of a man and wife from back in the early 1900's, the man was a hard-working husband and the wife a hard-working house wife, but the husband felt because he worked so hard to support their family that he was entitled to have an extra marital affair and went as far as to build his mistress a home on the same street as he and his wife and children lived on. Now that to me is conditional love on his part. I said that true story to a guy and his comment about the wife was "that was a strong woman" and my first thought was, "not strong but voiceless woman." She was aware of his misconduct and was probably taught loyalty over love which now our society is a product of our foremothers and forefathers leading by an unrewarding example. She may have been showing unconditional love for him or she may have been showing conditional love for herself, in not wanting to ruffle feathers since the husband was the sole provider, or the fear of not being able to meet anyone else in the future, or not wanting to uproot the children, or it could have been embarrassment. It could be any number of reasons why she stayed in the marriage, knowing that her husband was engaging in infidelity. I believe there should be standards that we should live by, and we should not accept any sort of behavior from those who say they love us.

Another form of conditional love is when one person in the relationship dominates his or her desires without ever considering the others involved. One example that comes to mind, a husband was married to his wife, and she claimed that they discussed having a family during the marriage, and each time the wife initiated the family conversation, the husband would just say, "now is not the time" and would put things off by saying "let's get our finances in order," or "let's build a larger home." Finally, after about five years of marriage, the wife called him on the carpet and wanted the truth, and he confessed that he did not want to have any children. Shortly, thereafter they divorced, and both moved on. There must be a conversation about children and how many children, with clear expectations, before the marriage, but seriously, who expects that from a spouse, especially if it had been discussed and an agreement made. I am sure, they loved each other…conditionally. He did not love her unconditionally enough to agree to having a child, and she did not love him unconditionally enough to continue the marriage without the chance to be a mother. There should be no assumptions when attempting to comingle lives together. It could be said that she wasted five years of a marriage and more while dating this guy and he knew all along how far he was going with not becoming a father in their marriage. When she told him why she was leaving, he made no effort to re-think his position to save his marriage and build a family. She now feels betrayed, misled, and unloved. The same could be said about his time and life wasted with someone that he thought he gave clear expectations of not being a parent. When there is no commitment and no compromise this equals conditional love. I have to say that she was the smart one in this instance, she did not just get pregnant and say tough, I'm pregnant and deal with it, because had she done that, it would have been tough alright, for her and the relationship with the child. Why bring children into this world where both parents are not in agreement on having a family.

If he told her from the very beginning that he did not want a family, he certainly stood by his words and like so many women have done, we think we can change a man's mind and who they are and persuade a man to do what we want. You cannot change a man or his mind. You can tell him how you feel and what you want until your face turns blue, and unless he has unconditional love enough to compromise then that man is going to do what he wants and when he wants. He may even decide to please you for a while or until his routine returns. This all goes back to not being fully committed. Not committed to any vows, relationship, standards, or each other.

I know there are a lot of stories of people who love each other, selfishly, and conditionally. When someone loves you unconditionally, the compromise is much easier.

I knew a man who wanted 6 or more children and would not compromise at all, as I think about it, he probably would have recanted his notion once he realized how expensive children are, from the diaper to the dorm there is endless expense and even beyond the dorm. It is important to seek out someone that is honest because people can and will tell you lies and tell you what they think you want to hear.

Conditional love may be normal for some step-children and step-parents so communication is very important when it comes to interacting with step-children. It is not practical to assume what your role and boundaries as a step-parent should be. It is best to have that possibly uncomfortable talk with the person that you are including into your life and be on one accord and consistent with how to interact with step-children and how to interact with the step-child's parents. Learn your place, and what boundaries you have set for you and the expectations of your spouse.

Thought

3

Immaturity

It is apparent to me that there are numerous levels of maturity in everyone, and it can fall under many categories like for some examples, there is a level of maturity when one decide to commit, or when you can appreciate or just plain notice the little things your spouse do daily, or when your spouse is saying one thing but mean another and you pick up on the meaning and not ignore or get angry but instead acknowledge your spouse's feeling and move forward.

They say that women are more mature than men by a few years, I could give the stats on the years, but by the time you read this, it will have changed. Keep that in mind when you are seeking a spouse that maturity is usually like fine wine, meaning it gets better with age, but that is not the case with everyone. There are some young dupes and old dupes. Do not give in to someone that may not be as mature minded as you try to be or as you think they should be, instead encourage them to do what makes sense for them as an individual or for the relationship. It is less stress on you and your spouse and less strain on the relationship.

Immaturity has many faces, it could be someone who swears or curses, someone who would rather pay the cable bill over the electric bill, someone with no goals or ambitions, someone who disrespects others, or someone who cares about outward appearance more than caring for their inner self, knowing when to speak and what to say to slow down a negative situation. They say to pick your battles. That means, every time someone says or does something that offends you, does not mean you have to get armored up to fight with them. Maturity is also letting some things go and being the person with integrity and not allowing someone to bring you back down from all the progress that you are making.

Thought

4

Single and Married not Much in Common

There may be some truth to what some have said, that married should associate with married or dating couples, and singles associate with singles. In most cases single people are on the prowl or are always trying to fill a void and are looking either for a commitment or a fling. It would not be wise for a man or woman to associate oneself with someone who is seeking a relationship, when the non-seeker is already in a relationship. You could become what you are around. I find that in some cases when a single person is having problems with someone that they are dating it can rub off on a stable marriage or relationship, of course, compiled with other relationship issues too, but certainly one of the factors is a questionable or unsteady relationship. You must be focused on what you want from the relationship, focus on your tolerances because we all have our limits and what one person will deal with, another person will not and that is what make us unique and where relationships succeed or fail. I have single and divorced acquaintances and I cannot think of one who was not bitter, even a little and that negativity and enviousness can attach like a magnet to a relationship that was okay and certainly one that was barely holding on to begin with. Even when associating with other married or dating couples, it is a good idea to gauge if one of the people in the other relationship may have wandering eyes or the potential to be unfaithful, because that is also not for a thriving marriage or relationship. It is best to find people to associate with that exhibit strong and positive vibes.

I had one friend whose marriage ended because of the husband's bold infidelity and now the husband wants her back and would make comments like "well your friend is still with her husband" and she would tell him "They are not guaranteed to stay together" or "She can stay and put up with what she wants to". Keep your troubles in your paradise. Ask yourself this question, "where do you live? "Answer: "345 Our Business Drive". In other words, keep your business on your street and in your house. I knew a lady who cheated on her husband and I could not figure out why and I never asked, nor will I ever because I am not her and I was not in their relationship and it wasn't my business. When you are married only the two of you can work things out or fall apart. As well as not spilling your dirty business to your friends, limit what you tell family as well because you will forgive your spouse and your friend or family will still be furious and have no idea why you put up with that man or woman. Part of the reason people stay in relationships that others say they would not be in is because everyone's level of tolerance is different, as individuals or as a couple. People have unspoken feelings or quirks and outspoken ways and habits. Usually, the same person that wags their hand at you for staying with a man who cheats for example, will be the same person who stays with a man who will not work, drop her off in her own car to her job and demand for dinner to be cooked when she gets off work, most likely something that you would not be able to tolerate in a man and stay with. In other words, every relationship has their ups and downs and have some things that will not be perfect, because an imperfect woman and an imperfect man equal an imperfect marriage or relationship and no one is perfect. Let us talk about cheating, which is considered more "acceptable cheating" to a spouse a fling, or an affair?! Well, it depends on the individual that you ask. I have heard some women say they could forgive a fling more than an affair. I have heard some women say that flings are more forgivable because he did not care about the other person, or it was a one-time thing. I can see that perspective and the perspective of the person who loathes affairs. It is competing with another woman, not that we have intentions to compete it just works out that way, even though the wife is primary. I have heard ladies say "He cheated on me with her? Look at her, she is too this or too that." It seems that cheaters never trade up, they always meet someone who has depreciated in value, compared to the spouse being cheated on. Betrayal is another factor hard to overcome, knowing that there has been lying and deceit to have that affair and for God knows how long. Once a person is caught cheating, it destroys all trust or belief that they could ever be trusted or truthful at any point. Another negative is how some affairs end up, with the other woman feeling that the wife is the intruder and that she is the new sheriff in town to take over the reins of the man. When all it could be is the idea and excitement of taking someone else's husband. At the end of the day, the life of a "Step-wife" aka (other woman) has two outcomes. 1) The husband only uses the other woman for one thing only, convenient sex and the other woman will not be part of his day-to-day life or 2) the other woman get the man she has been cheating with but it comes with interacting with his kids, interacting with the ex-wife, making breakfast, lunch, dinner, taking care of the bills, taking care of the home, cleaning, going to family events, scratching his back, having sex with him when you do not desire to or sex losing its excitement and becoming mundane. All those things a 'step-wife' may not consider, and remember, a wife and her husband has fallen in love and they have grown together and built their life together and shared life's milestones together. The other woman would not be able to part-take in any of that just because she has not created her own memories like the wife and husband has created with each other. It will not be meaningful to the "Step-wife" because she was not a part of his life in that capacity. Also, people who take someone's spouse usually does not have a great outcome. There is always conflict, either with the original wife or with the children from the marriage or the children from the other woman comingling with the children from the marriage. They say, "all that ends well, is well." There is nothing healthy or sound about destroying a marriage and family. People who break up a marriage, usually ends up remarrying or moving to other relationships over and over thinking that happiness is in another person, when happiness is within everyone, independent of sharing life with someone. Chances are that if someone cheats with you, they will cheat on you. Men who are cheated on by their wife, from a woman's perspective it is usually more than sex that is missing from the marriage. It is the emotional connection, trust, or being in love has faded away. I knew of another lady who cheated on her husband, and she told me why, it was because the husband was cheating and had cheated on her several times and a few times he even spent his whole paycheck on partying instead of bringing the money home to support his family. They lost their home and eventually got divorced, but not before bringing children in this world. Couples should seriously consider all the pros and cons before having a family. It destroys the children and their ability to cope with relationships and it skews their views on love and commitment. Everyone eventually moved on, but all the children from the marriage are living their life in an irresponsible manner, just as they witnessed as children.

Thought

5

Read the Signs

Do not ignore the obvious, my mother always taught me if a man will respect his mother, then he will respect you and it is true. I know there are some gentleman husbands out there, that speak and treat their wife as they speak and treat their mothers or daughters, with the utmost delicate respect, and those men must set the example for how their sons should speak and treat their mothers, sisters, and future spouse, in addition daughters should be shown how they should be spoken to and treated by their future spouse, by the way fathers speak and treat their wives. On the opposite side of the coin if a child is shown any violent misconduct both verbal or physical, this teaches them to behave in this way or to receive that type of brutality.

Much of what some people accept relates to our self-worth. There are some women that disrespect themselves and for these women as with anyone, you get out what you put in. Respect is earned and can be learned for the ones who are willing to learn. Some say you must demand respect that is true for the people who show respect as well. When you first start to date someone notice their behavior when someone makes them angry, watch their road rage, ask about previous relationships, watch as they interact with their child(ren) if they have any, or watch how they treat their parents or how they feel about them and gain some clues as to the problem that he or she may have or have had in the past that might hinder your new found relationship. Don't be afraid to analyze their response, not to be judgmental, but to get in tune with their character based from someone else they may have dated because after all you are a different person, however, watching these characteristics can give a clear view of what you may expect from this new person in your life. Ask tough questions have deep meaningful conversations and express yourself as well, the person you are dating may or may not like some of your views and maybe you have indifferent views on certain things but that is what set us apart as individuals. None of us will agree on everything but we can agree to disagree. Have a peaceful resolution to all or most disagreements, we should never get into a shouting match and encourage violence with anyone, it does not resolve any problems but only ignites more anger by saying or doing things you may later regret. Why say or do something that you cannot take back and that you may have to apologize for later. Watch out for people that always blames the other spouse for things not working out, because a lot of the times there are some blames on both parts. There are some cases where people are being taken advantage of and the spouse who is the giver are usually controlling and will stay in a relationship where they are dominant to the spouse receiving that sort of treatment. Keep an open mind and read between the lines. If you meet someone and they are single because they cheated on the last person, but they say something to excuse their infidelity, chances are they will cheat on you. It is natural for people to want to impress the other person when they are seeking a new relationship, so by telling you the other person is the reason they cheated, somehow in their heads, justifies cheating. Watch the friends that your companion associates with. Not all friends are terrible, but if the majority have questionable behavior that can mean one of two things, either the person you are interested in is a wolf in a sheep costume, or they are not selecting the right friends. Either way could be a red flag for negative influence. Listen to their family. Family knows that person better than you at this point. Don't involve your entire family in your personal quest, confide in someone that you are confident that can be trusted and trust your instincts.

Thought

6

Relationship Interview Questions

It is almost like being interviewed for a job; we hope a good relationship outlasts some jobs. You do not have to ask all the questions that you want answered all at once, however, get around to asking the questions that are appropriate for the significance of the relationship. Keeping your views in mind, next are a few important questions to ask, in no particular order.

Do you have a wife/husband? You may chuckle but this may save you from a going no-where relationship or breaking up an existing relationship.

Do you have a girl/boyfriend or fiancé? If they pause or say "it's complicated" then

KEEP IT MOVING. Things are already starting with deception, which is not how you want to begin your potential relationship.

What faith or spiritual belief do you associate with?

What are your views on religion?

Do you believe in God?

Do you pray?

If yes, how often do you pray?

Do you read the Bible?

If yes, how often do you read the Bible?

What are your personal goals?

What are your career goals?

How far are you from achieving your goals?

What is your relationship with your father or a father figure like?

What is the relationship with your mother or mother figure like?

Do you have children?

What is your relationship with your ex like? (Chances are if there is a problem with the ex, he/she may not have a good relationship with his/her children).

How often do you see your children?

Do you pay child support?

Is child support court ordered?

Are you in arrears? (This is important if you intend to move towards a life together, to purchase a home, or awareness of debt).

Do you want children (more children)?

How many children do you want?

What are your views on disciplining a child?

Do you live on your own / own your own home or plan to own a home?

If they live at home with parents, why? (Hard times or saving money may not be a deal breaker)

Do you save money?

What percent of your income do you save?

Do you pay bills on time?

Do you pay anyone else bills?

Have you traveled domestically or internationally?

Do you like to travel?

If yes, what are some places that you would like to travel or have traveled?

Do you owe taxes?

Have you cheated on an ex?

If yes, when, what, or why?

Do you use drugs?

Have you ever used drugs?

Do you smoke? How much/often?

Do you drink alcohol? How much/often?

Do you have student loan/credit card debt?

Do you like me as a friend or to build a future with?

What do you think of my children?

Do you think my children are well-behaved?

How do you view my way(s) of parenting?

Do you party or go to clubs? If so, how often?

Do you gamble? If so, how often?

What is a reasonable time to come home after hanging with your friends?

Do you plan to marry one day?

How long would you date someone before proposing?

How long would you be engaged before marrying?

Can you see yourself married to me?

If I pulled your record, what would I find? (Pull it, if your gut tells you)

Have you ever been accused of domestic violence?

Have you been on probation, prison/jail? If yes, for what?

Have you ever or do you drink and drive?

What is your occupation or what do you do for a living?

What do your friends do for a living?

If you lost your job, how long can you survive with no job?

If one job is not enough to sustain bills, what will you do?

If cohabiting or deciding to, who will handle paying the bills?

Do you prefer joint or separate bank accounts? Why or why not?

What type of decisions should we make together?

What type of decisions can we make independently?

Do you need space or time before settling an argument?

Do you prefer to address a disagreement on the spot?

Can we agree not to argue in front of our children or in public?

Can we argue without saying something regretful or being disrespectful?

Men should ask the women with child(ren):

How often does the child's father see their children, and if they say, the father does not care, investigate, or better yet allow her to continue talking, you may get the answer. You will see what kind of mother you may be interviewing for your future children.

Be ready for the answers and to act on the answers based on your needs or desires in a partner. The series of questions are some ideas and not meant to interrogate. Tailor questions for you. You know you best. You are important and who you choose to spend your life with and have a family with are important and is a great gauge to decide if this person is a fit for you or if you are a fit for them. You may not know the answers to the questions for your own life and may think, I cannot expect him or her to have answers that I do not have, but questions are a guide for you becoming more mindful or a better person and realizing that you are worthy of a decent person to help fulfill your life. Do not want this person so badly that you are willing to make excuses and accept them for the answers you get, or allow this person in your heart and you know they are not a God sent. Be prepared to keep it moving, if you are not spiritually, emotionally, physically, or financially able to deal with this person's baggage. Never ever date someone that is already in a relationship or married, because as I said before if they cheat with you, they will cheat on you. Starting a relationship with dishonesty blurs the level of trust and the relationship will be filled with insecurities based on how the relationship began, and likely not last. We all come with baggage, so the answers from your prospected partner from the questions that I listed or your personalized questions may not be a "deal breaker" but it is meant to be a knowledge meter to make a life decision to accept their baggage and intermingle with your baggage. Remember that often men will play in the sandbox but when it is time to select "the one" they usually get who they want, meaning they usually seek out the best woman for themselves, when they are really not worthy or up to her standards, and often times women settle either because of low self-esteem or because that man we settled on has a few broken wings that we think we can fix. We may know or have proof that he may be cheater, liar, disrespectful, and the list could go on, but we think we are that special woman that will glide into his life and suddenly he's not cheating, not lying, not being disrespectful, and going to marry you and then you are shocked and clutching your pearls when he does all of the above.

Thought

7

Do not Waste your Life

Maybe you are currently with someone that is not right for you, ask yourself if you are also right for them. Decide or know what you want from life and get the most you can out of it. There will be times when you feel as though you have wasted your life with someone that really was not right for you or you may not share similar goals or faith and that is okay if you are aware of what you are getting yourself into before you tie the knot or jump the broom. Communication is key if everyone is being honest about what is being communicated. Above all, being honest from the beginning is important for all involved. I knew of a woman who found this man who she thought was the "golden" one, and his gold points were that he had a good job, owned his home, and had a car. I told her, "You have all those things," why wouldn't any 40-year-old have a job, a car, and a home. After getting to know her and hearing her story, I learned that she did not have any good male role models. The men in her family did not work or at least not honest or consistent work and lived on their mom or girlfriends and they had no aspirations in life. When this "golden" guy came along, she thought he was her knight in shining armor. By all accounts he was part of the normal population that works for a living, not a self-made millionaire. Know what is acceptable and what is exceptional in a person. If you have the same or more than the person you are in a relationship with or seeking to be in a relationship with, that is an acceptable way of life and both of you should be striving for exceptional.

Thought

8

Boundaries Anyone?

Set boundaries and stick with them as closely as possible. When you meet a guy and he passes the "first interview" process and you each are communicating about your lives together, decide how much time you are willing to invest in that relationship, before you move on. I cannot tell you how many times I have met people that date for a decade or more and then complain to their friends or family or wonder why they are not married to this person that they have been with for over 10 years. First, you must ask your companion, if they would ever consider marriage, and know within your heart how long that you intend to wait or even if they are the right person, if it will take so long for a marriage.

I met a lady who complained that her boyfriend of over 10 years did not marry her and she felt like she wasted her life with this man, but had she had some boundaries in place, he would not have been able to lead her down that decade of her life or his life. Or, had they communicated about their futures, it would be understood this is not a relationship that will be headed down to the alter.

Dating in a long-term relationship does not mean automatic marriage. Do not assume that he is going to pop the question and you all will live happily ever after. Having a child with someone, does not trap a man or woman into automatic marriage. It only complicates things and hurts the woman who thought having a child or children would change the man's thinking into being an official family. Be honest about your intentions for the relationship, this goes for men as well. When my husband and I started dating and decided there was more to our dating, he asked how long I would date before I expected marriage, I answered about 2 or 3 years, and we got married 3 years to the day of our first date. It has not been easy for either of us, we have had our trials and triumphs like most relationships, but we have found a way to keep it together since January 1998. I would not have waited much longer if marriage was not on the menu. I had those standards prior to meeting him. There are people that decide to date over 5 years before marrying, these couples plan for the end goal of marriage but could be waiting to finish school or save for a lavish wedding, dream honeymoon, or a home.

Thought

9

Be Alone or Be Lonely

They say who wants to die alone and I say who wants to die lonely. Two different meanings entirely as a matter of fact we all will die alone and we each will meet our Maker on an individual basis. As for as being lonely I have personally encountered the feeling of loneliness while married and I am sure there may be some men and women that are dealing with the same but speaking from a woman's perspective, loneliness is having a house full of people and feeling like there is no one there for you emotionally, spiritually and in some cases physically. I use to fault people for leaving their children and spouses, until I was faced with emptiness, it is a void that no one can fill and I understand why some turn to addictions, it is only a temporary fix for those who do not have a support system, outlet or more importantly, a spiritual compass. It is horrible to feel that you cannot count on or trust anyone to talk to. You expect some distrust from frequently untrustworthy people however, one does not expect distrust or no loyalty from someone you have completely trusted to tell all your problems and short comings to. That is a lonely feeling and a reminder that God is the only one to trust with all your cares, because He cares for you. To be physically single, a widow, or divorced is not anything to show disdain towards. Being alone makes things much less complicated than being in a relationship. You only have you to answer to or blame for anything, you can only disappoint yourself, you can't be cheated on, you can't be yelled at, you can't be given the cold shoulder, you can drive how you want without critique, you can eat what you want without critique, you can watch whatever movie that you want without anyone else input, you can go where you want without any input, you can stay where you visited as long or short as you want without any input, you can buy what you want without any input, you can have only the company that you like or want coming over to your home without dealing with anyone else's family, you can say yes when you want, you can say no when you want. You do not have to consider anyone else's feelings or thoughts if you are completely alone. There are benefits to not being in a relationship, if you can handle being lonely at times.

Thought

10

Being Unequally Yoked

Mainly spiritually many learn the hard way that spiritual compatibility is essential to a marriage and it is as important as eating or sleeping in some instances, or at least date a person who believes as closely to what you believe because it will cause a conflict not only among each other but when it is time to start a family these views can pose huge problems when it is time to have a family and children. Another compatibility issue is financial not so much the need for a lavish lifestyle as much as the necessity of having similar goals in life regarding saving for your children's future, our own future, investments, stocks, or debt and the plan to decrease it. Some people live from check to check and I understand the necessity to live that way, for a while, but somehow, we must learn to work smarter for the future. A great example are immigrants, which some may have lived in poverty most of their adult lives and made a conscious decision to make a better life for themselves and send back for the family. Sex is another aspect of being equally yoked. I am sure the men that read this are shouting "Amen," but in all seriousness, conversations should be had about expectations and desires and willingness to meet or compromise on those expectations. You cannot expect for your spouse to know what you like and vice versa. Communication is the key to learning more about your spouse and meeting in the middle on decisions on sex-life together. There should be communication and consideration when it comes to pleasing your spouse. I usually have a saying that, "this road has a double yellow line, not a white line," which means there should be give-and-take outcome between couples, and should not go one person's way. If both parties think of the other person, then both will be happy and both needs will be met. The other person experiencing the shorter end of the stick will be miserable and eventually that misery will turn into pain and hurt, and then resentment, and retaliation.

Thought

11

No Tricks or Treats

You cannot sex your man into marriage. Have you heard the saying "why buy the cow, if you can get the milk free"? Sleeping in another room or downright not performing in bed, when you had been, will not put a ring on your finger. A man is a man, and you are setting the tone for him to find what he wants elsewhere. Stop asking him, "what are we going to do" when he is doing exactly what he wants to do. You have given him sex, a family, and the whole lifestyle all without marriage. You should not have to beg for marriage, when a man wants to marry you, he will let you know and will not let you go and will trip over himself to keep you. Unfortunately, some women make it difficult for a man to be in a serious relationship with you, because of your attitude, or vengeful ways. You take or share someone else's man and play games by ruining his reputation, filing false police reports, filing false restraining orders, withholding children that you both share, telling him it's his child when there is a chance it isn't, or telling him it's not his child when it is, slashing tires, keying cars, putting sugar in tanks, smashing windows to name a few, all because that man will not leave their main woman for you or because you are the main woman and he's cheating with someone else. And you want him to marry you? And why would you want to fight for someone that is incapable of being faithful? Why would he want someone with no dignity? You are worth more than that. Do not try to trick anyone to marry you by getting pregnant, that will back fire one way or another. Either he will not marry you, or he might marry you, because he feels pressured to, but will not be committed to the marriage, meaning he is still cheating with his mistresses or being disrespectful and blatantly not showing any consideration for your needs or feelings and with how he treats you.

Another couple I knew dated for about 15 years and the girlfriend decided after having a child with this man that she would move on, simply because he would not commit to marriage. I am sure there were other issues, but marriage may have sealed it for her to hang in there a bit longer.

Commitment is everything to some women and we give ample time for some of these men to commit.

Thought

12

Is Sex Overrated?

Sex plays a major role in a healthy relationship. Bad or unsatisfying sex is like a bad toupee you just get by or make do but you excessively fantasize about what you would rather do and for some who you would rather do. These stats may have changed, but I read once that over 70% of men and over 50% of women admitted to cheating on their spouse. Imagine how many more that did and will not admit it. Infidelity is a quick fix but that does not resolve the problems within the marriage and for a lot of couples the physical, emotional connection is gone. There is selfish sex or conditional love making, some are guilty of. Sex can be overrated in casual relationships because of the lack of the emotional connection and may not be overrated in a committed relationship because it should be an emotional connection. Women like to be "courted all day" or we add a level of feeling that is appealing when our man wash dishes, take care of laundry, get dinner started, help with the children, or just telling the wife to go and get a massage and your mani-pedi and take the kids to the park or movies. All those things are an aphrodisiac for women. We also like foreplay. Foreplay means to us that you care about taking time to please us outside of the act of sex. On the flip side, ask what your husband wants from you as well as conveying what you want. At the end of the day, it is the connection that makes it come together and often all we need is to bond with who we have chosen to be our partner.

Communication is a master key in relationships that all of us should hold; it will open every door in a relationship.

Thought

13

My Parents Said

Just because your mom or dad lived life the way they choose does not mean it will be right for you or that it will work for you. I believe that in some cases we spend our child hood one way and our adult and married life correcting the damage that our parents may have unintentionally bestowed on our lives. I have heard parents say to their children "you did not come with a manual; I am doing the best I can to raise you." and I imagine children would like to say "you didn't come with a manual either, I am doing the best I can to understand you". I wonder if raising children from an emotional perspective was worse for our fore mothers and fore fathers. Have they endured much more than our parents, or one cannot help but wonder how in the world did they survive all the emotional roller coasters of life without the professional help that is now available in abundance. Much like children with ADHD, or Autism. I do not think these diagnoses are new, they just put a name on some of the same behaviors. It could be that no one addressed it, or people just said, "oh that kid was dropped on his head, don't mind him" and people moved on. Or it was no big deal to address why someone did not learn like the other children, they were accepting of their child not having traditional education and started working at a young age and moved on with life. From this window view, things seemed to be much simpler then than they are now, in some ways.

Thought

14

You are not Going to Change Him or Her

One of the main issues in a relationship can be attempting to change the other person. There are things that someone who loves you will sacrifice for you, but they are who they are. They may appear to change, but given the right disagreement and stress, the person with real feelings will emerge. Not to say that no one can change, because they can, however, you cannot change them unless they have the desire to change from within. Often there are childhood traumas, abuse, or a social lifestyle that they grew up around that helps mold a person into who they are, those can be hard shells to crack. Or the person is simply "touched" in the brain and no amount of guidance corrects mental imbalance. Change can happen, most of the times it is maturity or a desire to seek more out of life. Another alternative for change is when a tragic event happens to ensure someone having a change of heart. Like if someone stops driving a vehicle under the influence, when they lose a loved one to a drunk driver. There are circumstances that compel people to change, but again it must be a desire from within.

Thought

15

Secrets or Not

When someone asks you, tell me what you like, tell them, but when they ask you what your dislikes are, give them general answers about what you may consider deal-breakers. Be careful on being specific about some of your dislikes, because there are what I like to call "chameleons" on the prowl that will attempt to morph into the person that you want them to be, until they get your heart, marry you, or have children with them. The real person will emerge, and you could feel like you do not know this person who has been in your life all this time. This may not be the case for everyone, there are some honest people in the world, and hopefully your instincts will guide you, but be alert because there are manipulators out there that prey on everything that you tell them and will become the persona that you disclosed to impress you. If you find yourself speaking freely about your dislikes, time will take care of the impostures. I believe dating someone for at least 6 months before considering being serious will reveal a lot about them. Something or someone will anger them, or they will become bored with getting to know you or exhausted from trying to keep up with this character that they have created. Or they could become distant with you and that is your glimpse into a longer-term life time with that person or they will move on and it becomes a blessing that they have moved on, even if you do not recognize it at a particular time in your life.

Thought

16

Watch and Listen to Body Language

So many times, I have witnessed women do things for all the wrong reasons, some to keep a man or to get a man. Body language can sometimes speak louder than words. When someone calls or text occasionally or never, meaning you are the one calling or texting, it is evident he/she is not that into you or at the very least, he/she may be preoccupied with someone else. When someone tells you that they are not in love with you, believe them. If someone does not show any sort of affection or affirmation towards you, keep it moving. It is nice to receive things for your birthday, Christmas, or Valentine's Day but random acts of kindness are essential in a relationship and it should not take a commercial holiday to be reminded to show that you care about someone. If someone that you are married to or dating shows that they care about you or even love you, means that person thought enough of you and was thinking of you and wanted to make you smile or make your day. This goes for both husbands and wives and those who are in relationships or seeking a relationship. Be the change you want in him/her, chances are they will follow suit. Even if it is unnoticed by your spouse, you should feel good about not having a negative and grumpy outlook on things in life. Pray for your spouse that God will give them grace and the will to meet you where you are.

Thought

17

Eyes Wide Open

If there are circumstances as to why you have moved in with someone that you want to spend your life with or marry, chances are things will not work out the way that you have envisioned. I read about a woman who moved a guy in, and he told someone else that he moved with her because he was hungry. Another woman moved in with a guy, because her home needed repair. It was not that they were so in love and both could not be apart from one another one more day. This same guy that moved the woman in his home, did not want her to buy anything or decorate his home. That says a lot to me. He really wanted to just help her out and for her to save money to move out. He had been a bachelor and he was okay with that lifestyle. Do not force yourself into a woman or man's life. You will not be treated like you were a precious jewel that was purposefully pursued but you will likely be treated like a stray cat, figuratively fed once a week, not taken to family events, not introduced to family, not included in important decisions, not truly being a part of someone's life or claimed as belonging to each other.

Thought

18

Listen to the Silence, you may Hear the Clues

As much as you listen to what comes out of someone's mouth, you must also listen to what you do not hear; like body language. Body language is where someone spends their time, money, and who they spend time with. Also, spirituality or lack thereof speaks. Everything in life and of life that is without sound can speak to us. We must listen to the sound of life's clues.

Another example of listening to unspoken clues is relationship baggage. In many cases, unless you are young and new to dating most mature folks who has lived a little in life is not undetached from someone. There is either residual baggage, active baggage or plain old will not let go baggage. Either way, prepare for how you intend to handle someone whom you may have an interest in and they had an interest in you, as to how they move on from that past relationship or linger with the past relationship. It tells you they may not be over that person, especially if there is no real effort to avoid the person in the previous relationship. Even if children are in the equation, there should still be limited interactions with your child(ren)'s mother or father, like what time are you picking Billy or Sally up or what time will you be dropping Suzy or Cody off or notifying your child that their mother or father is on the phone, on their way, or at the door. At no time should there be any hanging out at the ex's house for milk and cookies or reminiscing on old times. In most instances if the ex was such a keeper, you would not have moved on. Whoever messed up or for whatever reason that the relationship with your ex ended, keep it ended and show respect and dignity toward your new relationship.

Thought

19

What to Do?

If you have experienced even a few of the things mentioned in the previous thoughts or chapters, it may be time to self-evaluate your life. Your life. That is just what it is. Take charge of your life, in a diplomatic way. Do not be angry with your partner, change what you want for yourself. After all, you hold the master key to being content. Accept being with someone or without someone, even if it is just for a season.

Thought

20

Public Service Messages

I know we like to have someone to bounce ideas and life's issues with. At the end of the day God is the only being that can change anything. Talk to God about your problems. Sometimes friends and family will lead you astray, either for selfish reasons or because they do not know any better. God will never fail you and you will not hear about it later and how and what you say will not get twisted when you give your cares to the Lord.

Single folks ask the Lord to send you a spouse but if you do sin, please do not have unprotected sex. Would you eat food or drink from a filled or empty biohazard container? No, not even if it was your own waste.

Ladies do not attempt to trap a man by having a child(ren) with him. You will be tethered to that child or those children for the rest of yours and his/her life.

Do not stray from your goals. A good man/woman will support you and a smart woman/man will join in achieving their own goals.

Thought

21

Ladies and Gentlemen

You have got to know when to hold him/her and fold her/him! No one is perfect, but do not waste your life away if you do not get close to what you want out of a relationship, much like when you have a specific food, clothing, car or buying a home, we rarely settle when we invest our money in material things. You should rarely settle, when investing and comingling your life and time in a relationship, because you are valuable and more important than material things. I knew a woman who was with a guy for nearly 10 years and he basically told her that he did not want to label their relationship and did not want her to date anyone else; and by the way, he was dating other women and stated he did not want to guarantee that he would be faithful. At some point, I advised her that if I were in her shoes, I would run and never look back, no matter the time that I invested, because at the end of the day, you are worth being happy, you are worth the peace that you seek and all we have is time, why not be a good steward of your time until God says it is our time to leave this earth.

I knew of another woman who is now married, but the husband did not marry her for 10 years and he was cheating all those years and he is still cheating after marriage, and it is rumored that she is also cheating. It appears that love have little to do with that union. I do not know about you, but a casual and loveless marriage is not worth the trouble of all that it entails, like raising children, working to live, and building a future together. I realize there are people that marry for convenience. Like the benefit of medical or life insurance or for someone to help with living expenses. It is not the union of marriage as God intended it to be and it is unethical and a travesty.

Yes, there are compromise in relationships because no one is alike, but compromise should be practical and close to effortless when you sincerely commit to one another. The compromise should never be, oh well he/she does not want to commit or marry so I will accept that until usually whenever they are old and grey or no one else want them or if you come into money. Even having children together without marriage, no matter how it is accepted, it is still backwards behavior and not the way God intended. Why would someone that cares more about themselves do anything for you, like marry or commit when you already live together, have a "family". There is no journey in that, you have already arrived at the destination, the destination of being together for many years without any communal value. Be careful who you allow in your life for your children's sake. It has been said that a woman cannot raise a man and vice versa and I say just because there is a man or woman in the home does not equate an automatic positive influence. There have been many stories of a person seeking companionship or happiness in a relationship and brought into their home a person with baggage's of alcoholism, molestation, or abuse to name a few. All men or women do not have the best intentions with you or your children.

Thought

22

Say what you Mean and Mean What you Say

Never lead someone in to thinking you are doing one thing but have another agenda. Always be honest about your wishes and your feelings. Chances are you will gain and always be respected for your honesty. There is a delicate way to say anything, there is no need for fussing, cursing, and losing control. Always, practice exercising self-control in all endeavors, with your spouse, children, boss, co-workers or that person that cut you off while driving no matter what someone say or do to you. If you react to foolish behavior, you get nowhere in a hurry and it usually does not resolve anything, it intensifies and makes the other person react poorly as well. Practice not saying or doing anything that you will have to apologize for later. If you request for a change in your partner, don't back out on it, just because you get sweet talked, sweet gifted or sweetly made love to, it's all a trick for the most selfish one to get what they want, where you are ALWAYS the one to compromise. If you give in, you are setting a trend that the other person in your relationship will notice and play that same tune on the same fiddle, each time you demand for change.

Thought

23

Meet in the Middle

There is no shame in meeting in the middle, as a matter of fact, it is essential. Having a conversation where you have a meeting of the mind. You do not have to be stubborn just to prove a point and not compromise, just simply ensure that your partner is giving you something that you want, if you give them something that they want. Decisions between partners goes both ways and not just one way. There must be a give and take, not only take-take or give-give. Not meeting in the middle is a sure way to walk the hamster wheel of a relationship, which goes nowhere. I am the first to admit that I can be your best friend if you do not push my buttons. Learn your spouse, do not stir up the ant mound without the antidote to treat the mound. Do not create or bring a problem to a situation without a solution. Or, at least work together on a plan of action when there is trouble in parasite, I meant paradise.

Thought

24

The Value of your Time

Spend daily time with God! Talk to God as often as you can whenever you can. It is a great stress reliever to know that you can be honest when you pray. Spend time alone, and tell your spouse or kids, this is my time, I will not be doing anything but whatever I desire for the next 30-60 minutes. Exercise is another stress reliever and find things that you and your spouse may enjoy together, like a hobby, comedy shows, movies, hiking, walking, sharing ideas, literally anything. I take our children to the movies often and I cherish those moments with them. I love love love going to the movies, ALONE. I like the peace of ordering whatever size buttered popcorn and cherry cola I want. Not hearing commentary of the movie while on the screen. Some men must unwind after work or after moving from the recliner to the couch to watch sports or spend time with their friends, women also need to carve out time outside of doing laundry, cooking, cleaning, helping children with homework and other daily activities and find alone time to revitalize and recharge to start over for the next day.

My

Closing

"Thoughts"

Respect your spouse. Respect your parents. Respect your in-laws and family. Single parents respect your child(ren)'s mother or father. After all you chose that man or woman to make a child(ren) with or they chose you. Show respect for and around your children. Most of all respect yourself. If you respect you, you will respect all others.

Just as various technologies of computer systems can be fantastic until there is an error, people can be terrific until they do or say something terrible. Expect the wheel of your relationship to need a squirt of oil once in a while. We all make mistakes with one another as we do our Heavenly Father. Forgive one another and learn from the mistakes made.

Question:

Do you have The Life of a Step-Wife?

SPECIAL THANKS

Special thanks to my two accountability coaches. My dad, Carl Jackson Jr. and oldest son Ramzi. My dad and son would ask me regularly, "Where are you with your book?" Well coaches, here it is.

Thanks to Ramsey, Ramzi, Chaz, and Jaycee for being integral parts of my journey.

www.ingramcontent.com/pod-product-compliance
Lightning Source LLC
Chambersburg PA
CBHW070854050426
42453CB00012B/2203